GW00367195

Theory of Music Workbook

for Trinity Guildhall written examinations

Grade 5

by Naomi Yandell

Published by:
Trinity College London
89 Albert Embankment
London SE1 7TP UK

T +44 (0)20 7820 6100
F +44 (0)20 7820 6161
E music@trinityguildhall.co.uk
www.trinityguildhall.co.uk

Designer and editor: Natasha Witts
Music processed by New Notations London
Printed in England by Halstan & Co. Ltd, Amersham, Bucks

Grade 5 Theory of Music Syllabus from 2007

Section 1	General multiple choice – 10 questions	*(10 marks)*
Section 2	Writing scales, arpeggios, broken chords	*(15 marks)*
Section 3	Correcting mistakes or setting words to a rhythm	*(10 marks)*
Section 4	Transposition	*(15 marks)*
Section 5	4-part chords for SATB	*(15 marks)*
Section 6	Adding a bass line to a tune or vice versa	*(15 marks)*
Section 7	Analysis – 10 questions	*(20 marks)*

Questions and tasks may cover all matters specified in previous grades and also the following:

Rhythm and form

1. Time signatures of $\frac{4}{2}$, $\frac{6}{4}$ and $\frac{7}{4}$
2. Time signature changes within an extract
3. Rules for grouping note and rest values within new time signatures (including grouping indications at the beginning of bars or scores, e.g. 2,3 or 3,2)
4. Grouping demisemiquavers in simple and compound time
5. Semiquaver triplets
6. The breve
7. Strophic, Verse and Refrain (or Chorus) and binary forms

Pitch

1. Naming and using notes in tenor clef
2. Ab, Db, E and B major keys (for all major keys for the grade: scales, key signatures, one-octave arpeggios, broken chords and tonic triads (root, first or second inversion)
3. F, Bb, C# and G# minor keys (for all minor keys for the grade: scales – natural (Aeolian mode) and harmonic and melodic, key signatures, one-octave arpeggios, broken chords and tonic triads (root, first or second inversion)
4. Identifying the key of a piece in Ab, Db, E or B major, and F, Bb, C# or G# minor
5. 2nd degree of the major/minor scale being known as the supertonic (and re for major keys)
6. Supertonic triads for all keys covered so far
7. Major/minor supertonic triad labelled:
   – as a chord symbol above the music (e.g. Dm in the key of C major or B dim (or B°) in the key of A minor
   – as a Roman numeral below the music (e.g. ii in the key of C major or ii° (dim) in the key of A minor)
8. Recognising some imperfect cadences
9. Double sharps and double flats and general enharmonic equivalent
10. Recognising and writing C and G pentatonic major scales
11. Inversions of all intervals covered in Grades 1-4 within an octave
12. Recognising and writing accented passing notes and understanding acciaccatura, appoggiatura, upper and lower mordents and trills
13. Understanding upper and lower auxiliary notes
14. Writing tonic, supertonic, subdominant, dominant or dominant 7th chords in root, first or second inversions in any key for the grade as well-balanced four-part chords for SATB
15. Transposing a tune up or down any major, minor or perfect interval within an octave (within the keys for the grade) or for transposing instruments for the grade
16. Ranges of the alto saxophone in Eb and trumpet and clarinet in Bb as defined in the workbook
17. Concept of modulation
18. Identifying a modulation to the dominant or the relative major/minor keys

Musical words and symbols

Dynamic and articulation marks
Pedal signs for piano/keyboard, *sotto voce*, *una corda*, (and signs and abbreviations for these where appropriate)

Tempo, expression marks and other words and signs
Agitato, arpeggiando, con forza, energico, grave, larghetto, appassionata, fuoco, morendo, niente, quasi, risoluto, rubato, scherzando, secondo, stringendo, tempo guisto

Introduction

Using this workbook

The writing in the boxes [ ] tells you:

- About the music that you sing, or play on your instrument
- What you need to know to pass your Trinity Guildhall Grade 5 Theory of Music examination. Topics from previous grades of the syllabus should also be known

Doing the tasks

- Use a pencil with a sharp point and a fairly soft lead so that you can easily rub out what you have written if you need to
- Be careful to be accurate with musical notes and signs – this will make a difference to your marks because the examiner must be able to read what you have written
- Read through the boxes to make sure you understand how to do the tasks and ask for help if you need it
- The first task in each section has usually been done for you in blue to show you what to do
- Use the picture of the piano keyboard on page 71. It is there to help you, even if you do not play a keyboard instrument
- **Always try to play, sing or tap the music you write.** This is a very important part of learning, and will help you 'hear' what you write in your head. It will help you in the examination when you have to work in silence

What comes next?

When you have finished this book try some sample papers. You can download them from www.trinityguildhall.co.uk (follow the links to Theory from the Music page). You will then be ready to ask your teacher to enter you for the Grade 5 Theory of Music examination.

Acknowledgements

Trinity Guildhall would like to acknowledge the invaluable contribution to the development of this music theory programme by music teachers, professors, examiners, language specialists and students from around the world. Their comments have usefully informed the final shape of the workbooks and examination papers, and are gratefully appreciated.

Tenor clef

Remember

The middle of any C clef centres on **Middle C**.

In Grade 4 you learned how important it is to be accurate when positioning the alto clef on the stave because there are other C clefs centred on different lines.

The new clef for Grade 5 is the **tenor clef**. Notice that it is centred one line higher than the alto clef.

Middle C

Here is **Middle C** written in bass, tenor, alto and treble clefs:

The tenor clef is used for instruments whose music tends to be written at the bottom of the treble clef stave and the top of the bass clef; using the tenor clef means that there is no need for the composer to write lots of leger lines.

Music for cello, bassoon and trombone is often written in tenor clef. Here is some music for cello written in both tenor and bass clefs to show why it makes sense to use the tenor clef here:

Telemann

1 Name these notes:

A♭   __   __   __   __   __   __   __

2 Write either a tenor or bass clef before these notes to make the note name correct.

G♯   F   F   B♭   D   A♯   E♭   G

3 Write either a treble, alto, tenor or bass clef before these notes to make the note name correct.

Eb F G# Eb B Ab D E

Handy tip!
Use **Middle C** to help you check your first and last note.

4 Write the following tunes using tenor clef, so that they sound at the same pitch.

Traditional (Scottish)

Traditional (American)

Handy tip!
Notice the position of the sharps or flats in the key signatures in tenor clef.

Telemann

Holst

etc.

Note values and rests

Demisemiquavers

Composers sometimes write:

 a demisemiquaver (worth half a semiquaver)

Like semiquavers, they can be beamed together in different ways. They are often beamed together in groups of four where the beat is a quaver:

Or like this where the beat is a crotchet:

or

or

Or like this where the beat is a dotted crotchet:

or

or

> **Handy tip!**
> Where three examples are given, the first two are the clearest and either of these should be used for your exam.

If composers write fewer than four demisemiquavers, they will also probably need to use a semiquaver or demisemiquaver rest. This is because notes and rests should be grouped in the beat of the bar (whether quaver, crotchet, dotted crotchet or minim).

Here is a demisemiquaver rest:

Here are some examples.

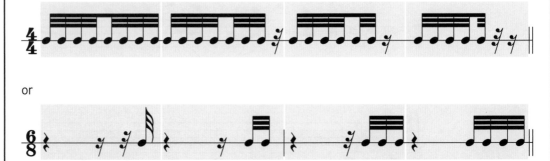

or

> **Handy tip!**
> Semiquavers and demi-semiquavers are also often beamed together like this where the beat is a quaver.
>
>
>
> or

Do not use two demisemiquaver rests one after the other, except where each rest completes the beat of the bar:

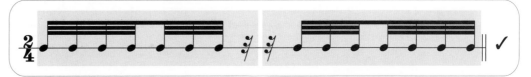

As with semiquaver rests, demisemiquaver rests are sometimes put inside the groupings of the bar to make the music easier to read:

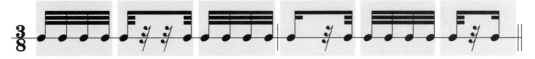

Here is a dotted semiquaver:

The dotted semiquaver is often followed by a single demisemiquaver because together they make up one quaver beat:

More rarely the demisemiquaver comes first:

Here is a dotted semiquaver rest:

1 Fill the coloured boxes with correctly grouped demisemiquavers. :

2 Fill the coloured boxes with correctly grouped rests.

3 Write correctly grouped rests below the asterisks (*).

4 Write 2-bar rhythms using the note values and rests you know. Include one dotted
  semiquaver note.

Semiquaver triplets

Sometimes composers want to divide a quaver beat into three equal parts. To do this
they write **semiquaver triplets** – three semiquavers to be played in the time of two.

For example:

Where the beat is a dotted crotchet, semiquaver triplets are grouped like this
(nine to be played in the time of six):

Where the beat is a crotchet and there are two semiquaver triplets one after the other,
they can be written like this (six to be played in the time of four):

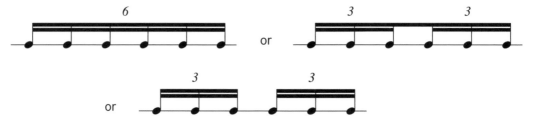

As with quaver triplets, sometimes composers want to use rests within triplet groupings.
You must bracket all semiquaver triplets where a rest is included in the triplet grouping.

1 Write some semiquaver triplets to agree with each time signature.

2 Add correct time signatures to the music.

Mozart

Janáček

Lizogub

Schubert

3 Add appropriate rests in the places marked by an asterisk (*) to complete the bars.

4 Using semiquaver triplets, write a broken chord using the appropriate triad. Use patterns of three notes each time. Finish no more than two leger lines above or below the stave.

Chord V in F major going down

Chord IV in G major going up

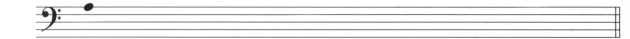

Chord i in A minor going down

Chord iv in D minor going up

New time signatures

For Grade 5 you need to know the following new time signatures:

$\frac{6}{4}$ (2 dotted minim beats in each bar)

$\frac{7}{4}$ (7 crotchet beats in each bar)

$\frac{4}{2}$ (4 minim beats in each bar)

$\frac{6}{4}$ is different from $\frac{3}{2}$ because its beats are grouped into two main dotted minim beats, not into three minim beats. This means that $\frac{6}{4}$ is a compound time signature because each dotted minim beat easily divides into three crotchets. For example:

(dotted minim beat easily divides into 3 crotchets)

(minim beat easily divides into 2 crotchets)

When writing in $\frac{7}{4}$ composers tend to group the crotchet beats into two or three longer main beats. These main beats are irregular in length, as they are in $\frac{5}{4}$.

Here are some examples:

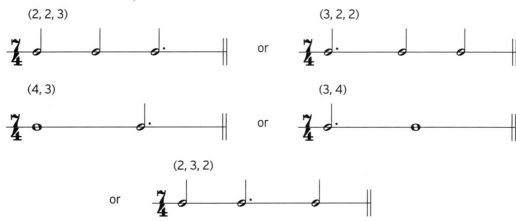

$\frac{4}{2}$ has four minim beats in each bar. When a note lasting a full bar is needed in this time signature a note called a breve is used: 𝄀𝅜𝄀

Here is a breve rest: ▬

Handy tip!

The coloured boxes help you to think in the main beats of the bar, whether dotted minim or minim.

Remember

Numbers are sometimes written above the music to show how notes and rests are to be grouped and beamed.

Remember

Semi means half so **semibreve** means 'half a breve'.

1 Write the main beats in each of the following bars:

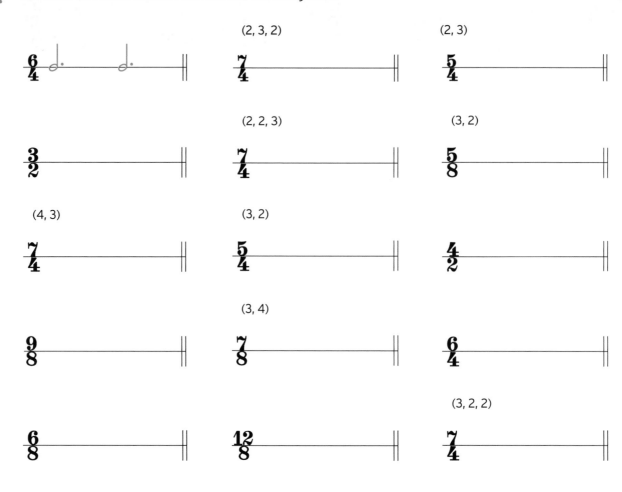

2 Write the correct time signatures.

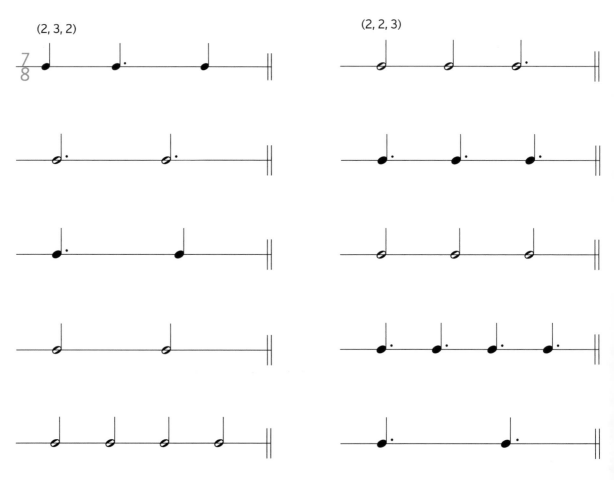

3 Add a time signature to each bar that is marked with an asterisk (*). The first four have been done for you.

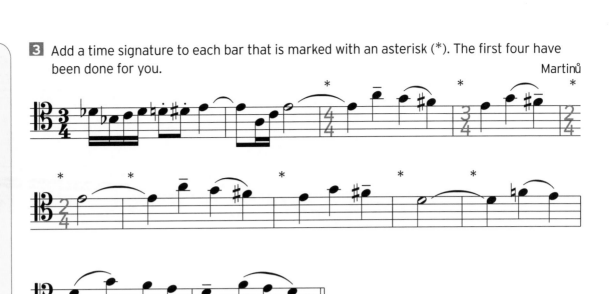

Martinů

Bartók

Mikrokosmos, sz 107 © Copyright 1940 by Hawkes & Son (London) Ltd. Reproduced by permission of Boosey & Hawkes Music Publishers Ltd.

Maxwell Davies

Violin Concerto © 1990 Chester Music Limited, 14-15 Berners Street, London W1T 3LJ, United Kingdom.
All Rights Reserved. International Copyright Secured. Reprinted by permission

Holst

Saxton

The Circles of Light © 1990 Chester Music Limited, 14-15 Berners Street, London W1T 3LJ, United Kingdom.
All Rights Reserved. International Copyright Secured. Reprinted by permission

Martinů

11

Holst

Berg

4 Look at the following music. Add bar lines to agree with the time signatures.

Scriabin

Lutosławski

Chain 2 © Copyright 1988, 1996 Chester Music Limited, 14-15 Berners Street, London W1T 3LJ, United Kingdom for the World Excluding Poland, Albania, Bulgaria, the territories of former Czechoslovakia, Rumania, Hungary, the whole territory of the former USSR, Cuba, China, North Vietnam and North Korea, where the copyright is held by Polskie Wydawnictwo Muzyczne – PWM Edition, Kraków, Poland. All Rights Reserved. International Copyright Secured. Reprinted by Permission.

Prokofiev

Piano Sonata no. 6, op. 82 © Copyright 1941 by Boosey & Hawkes Music Publishers Ltd. For the UK, British Commonwealth (Ex Canada), Eire and South Africa. Reproduced by permission of Boosey & Hawkes Music Publishers Ltd.

Shostakovich

Piano Trio no. 1, op. 8 © Copyright 1925 by Boosey & Hawkes Music Publishers Ltd. For the UK, British Commonwealth (Ex Canada), and Eire. Reproduced by permission of Boosey & Hawkes Music Publishers Ltd.

Remember

Composers often change clefs in a piece — sometimes in the middle of a bar.

Writing your own tunes to a given rhythm

1 Write a tune for violin using the first five degrees of the scale of C major to the given rhythm. Use a key signature and finish on the dominant.

Handy tip!
For a reminder of instrument ranges see page 70.

2 Write a tune for viola using the notes of the tonic triad in E flat major to the given rhythm. Use a key signature and finish on the tonic.

Remember
Add dynamics and articulation markings to make your music more interesting.

3 Write a tune for oboe using the first five degrees of the scale of A major to the given rhythm. Use a key signature and finish on the tonic.

(2, 3, 2)

4 Write a tune for guitar using the notes of the tonic triad in E minor to the given rhythm. Use a key signature and finish on the dominant.

5 Look at the tunes you have written and add some musical words and symbols that you know. Also see page 53 for those for Grade 5.

Setting words to a rhythm

1 Continue the rhythms to fit the following phrases.

The soldier on the battlefield may fight and run away,
But the miners in the powder smoke do work both night and day.
(English folk song)

Remember

For your exam you must put important words (or syllables) on strong beats in the bar.

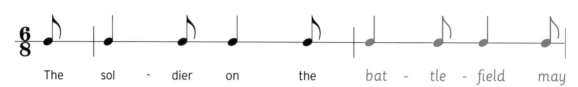

Handy tip!

You will see that each phrase is to be set in more than one way because it is possible to set the same words to rhythms in different time signatures.

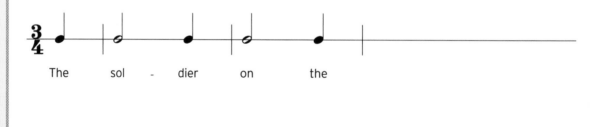

14

Draw near my friends and neighbours,
Good news to you I'll bring.
The fame of Admiral Nelson
From shore to shore to sing.
(English ballad)

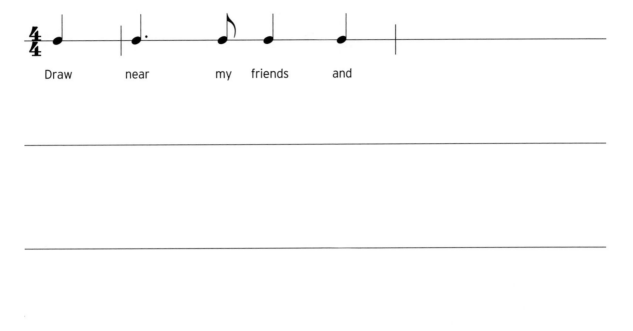

Draw   near   my   friends   and

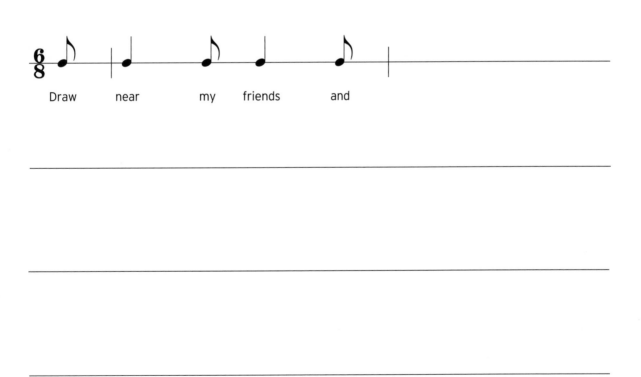

Draw   near   my   friends   and

2 Write a rhythm to fit each of the following phrases.

If you wake at midnight, and hear a horse's feet,
Don't go drawing back the blind, or looking in the street.
(Kipling)

_____

_____

_____

_____

The wrinkled sea beneath him crawls;
He watches from his mountain walls,
And like a thunderbolt he falls.
(Tennyson)

_____

_____

_____

_____

Pentatonic major scales on C and G

Handy tip!

Just as the pentagon is a shape with five sides, the pentatonic major scale is a scale with five notes.

A **pentatonic major scale** is made up of five notes and is played like a major scale without the 4th and 7th degrees. Music that uses just the notes of the pentatonic major scale is said to be in the **pentatonic major**. Many folk songs and spirituals are composed using the pentatonic major scale.

For Grade 5 the only pentatonic major scales that you need to know are those starting on **C** and **G**. Here they are:

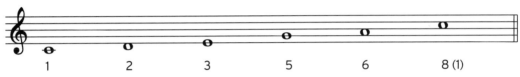

C pentatonic major scale

G pentatonic major scale

There are no semitones in either scale. This means that they are good scales to improvise with because there will be no clashes of a semitone.

Did you know?

There is no need to use a key signature for the pentatonic major scale on **G** because (unlike the **G** major scale) there are no **F**s in the scale.

1 Write a one-octave C pentatonic major scale in crotchets going up then down.

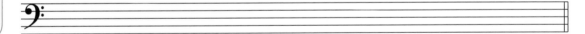

2 Write a one-octave G pentatonic major scale in minims going down then up.

3 Write 4-bar tunes using notes from the C pentatonic major scale. Write them in two 2-bar phrases with the first phrase finishing on **G** and the second on **C**.

4 Write 4-bar tunes using notes from the G pentatonic major scale. Write them in two 2-bar phrases with the first phrase finishing on **D** and the second on **G**.

5 Write an ostinato using notes from the C pentatonic major scale to accompany the pentatonic major tune **Swing Low, Sweet Chariot**.

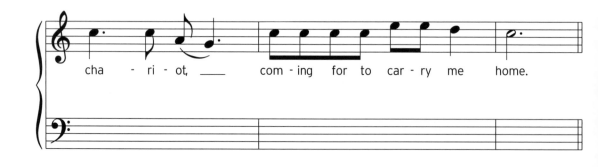

The circle of 5ths

Here is the circle of 5ths that you will recognise from Grades 1-4. The highlighted keys are the keys that you will need for Grade 5.

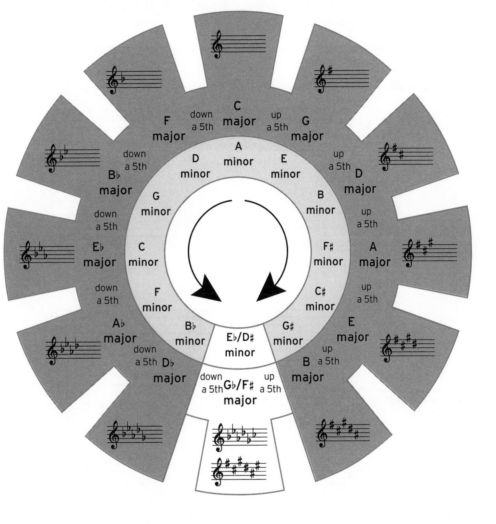

Using the circle of 5ths above, answer these questions:

1 Which minor key has four flats in its key signature?_____

2 Which major key has five sharps in its key signature?_____

3 Which minor key has four sharps in its key signature?_____

4 Which major key has four sharps in its key signature?_____

5 Which major key has five flats in its key signature?_____

6 Which minor key has five sharps in its key signature?_____

7 Which major key has four flats in its key signature?_____

More about the new keys for Grade 5

The new keys for Grade 5 are **E, B, A flat** and **D flat majors** (and their relative minors **C sharp, G sharp, F** and **B flat minors**). They work like the others you have learned; the key signatures are there to make sure that the tone-semitone pattern is the same for each key.

1 Write the key signature and the tonic triad in root position for each of the following keys.

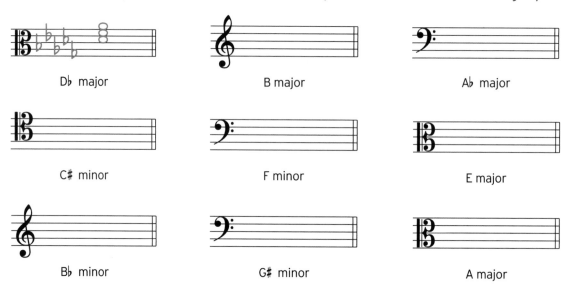

Db major   B major   Ab major

C# minor   F minor   E major

Bb minor   G# minor   A major

2 Write a one-octave B flat harmonic minor scale in minims ascending then descending. Use a key signature.

Did you know?

Ascending means 'going up'. **Descending** means 'going down'. In your exam these terms could be used.

3 Write a one-octave B major scale in crotchets descending then ascending. Use a key signature.

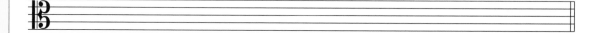

4 Write a one-octave E major scale in minims going down then up. Do not use a key signature but write in the necessary accidentals.

5 Write a one-octave D flat major scale in crotchets going up then down. Use a key signature.

6 Write a one-octave B flat harmonic minor scale in minims ascending then descending. Use a key signature.

7 Write a one-octave C sharp melodic minor scale in crotchets going up then down. Use a key signature.

8 Write a one-octave A flat major scale in crotchets ascending then descending. Do not use a key signature but write in the necessary accidentals.

G sharp minor and the double sharp

You have not yet written **G sharp minor** (relative minor to B major). Here it is in its natural, melodic and harmonic forms:

G# natural minor scale

G# melodic minor scale

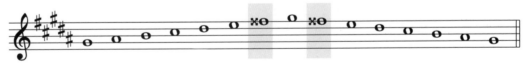

G# harmonic minor scale

Notice the accidental ✕ that is used where the 7th degree is raised by a semitone. This is a **double sharp** and it is needed because the 7th degree in G sharp minor is already **F sharp**. To raise it, it needs to be sharpened further. **F double sharp** is enharmonically equivalent to **G**, but writing **G** here would be incorrect.

1 Write a one-octave G sharp harmonic minor scale in minims descending then ascending. Use a key signature.

2 Write a one-octave G sharp melodic minor scale in crotchets going up then down. Use a key signature.

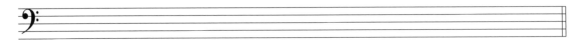

3 Write a one-octave G sharp natural minor scale in crotchets going up then down. Use a key signature.

Handy tip!

To start with, use a keyboard or the picture of the keyboard on page 71 to help you, and don't forget to look at the clef.

4 Circle the pairs of notes that are enharmonically equivalent.

  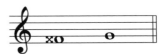

 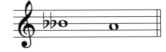 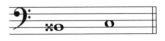

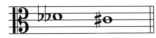  

  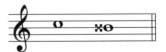

5 Write enharmonic equivalents of the following notes.

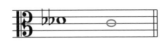 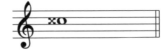 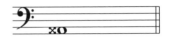

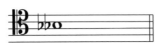 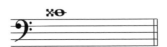 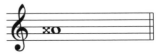

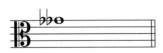 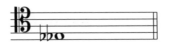 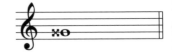

Labelling scales

1 Label these scales.

C# melodic minor going up (or ascending)

Remember

Melodic and natural minor scales sound the same going down, so either label is correct.

2 Label these scales. Here there are no key signatures so check the accidentals instead.

Arpeggios

1 Write the key signature for each key shown. Then write its one-octave arpeggio in the rhythm given below.

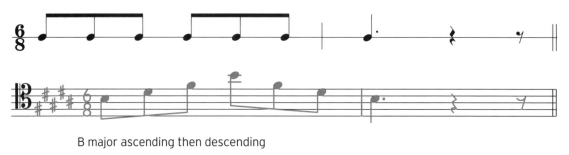

B major ascending then descending

C sharp minor descending then ascending

G sharp minor ascending then descending

A flat major descending then ascending

2 Label these one-octave arpeggios.

Working out the key of a piece

For Grade 5 you need to be able to recognise more major and minor keys (see page 19).
Here are two examples to remind you how to work out the key each time.

1

Beethoven

- Are there flats or sharps in the key signature and, if so, how many? *Yes, four flats, so the key could be A flat major or F minor*

- Are there any accidentals in the music that could be the raised 6th or 7th degrees in the relative minor? *No*

- Are there any other reasons to think that the key is A flat major? *Yes, the music is based around the tonic and dominant triads of A flat major*

Answer: *The key is A flat major*

2

J S Bach

etc.

- Are there flats or sharps in the key signature and, if so, how many? *Yes, four sharps, so the key could be E major or C sharp minor*

- Are there any accidentals in the music, that could be the raised 6th or 7th degrees in the relative minor? *Yes (so the key is probably a minor)*

- Are there any other reasons to think that the key is C sharp minor? *Yes, much of the music is based around the tonic triad in C sharp minor*

Answer: *The key is C sharp minor*

1 Use the questions above to work out the keys.

Mahler

Key: _____

Haydn

Key: _____

J S Bach

etc.

Key: _____

Chopin

etc.

Key: _____

Brahms

etc.

Key: _____

J S Bach

Key: _____

26

Transposing tunes up or down

Remember

Melody means 'tune'. In your exam this term could be used.

For Grade 5 you need to know how to transpose a melody by any major, minor or perfect interval within an octave.

Use the following method:
- Write the tonic of the piece and its key signature.
- Move the tonic up or down the required interval to find the new tonic.
- Write the new tonic and its key signature.
- Write out the tune up or down the required interval with the same intervals between the notes.
- Check that the last note that you write is the required interval higher (or lower) than the original last note.

1 Transpose the following melodies down a minor 2nd.

Remember

Use a key signature and add accidentals where necessary to keep the intervals the required distance apart.

Schubert

Beethoven

2 Transpose the following melody up a minor 2nd.

Beethoven

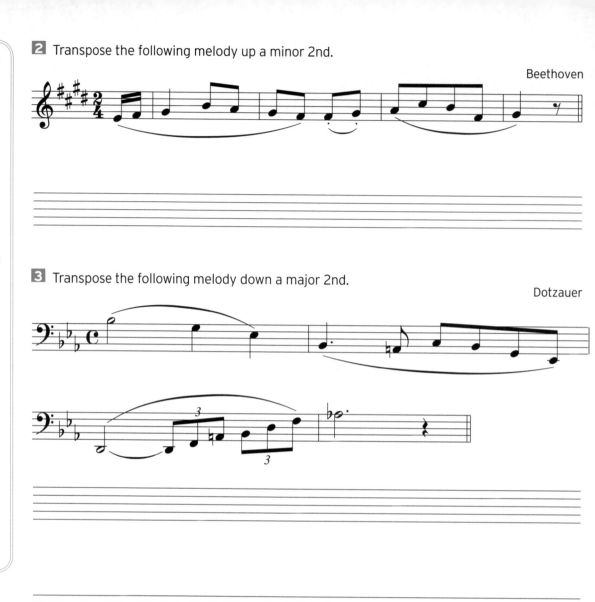

3 Transpose the following melody down a major 2nd.

Dotzauer

4 Transpose the following melody up a major 2nd.

Beethoven

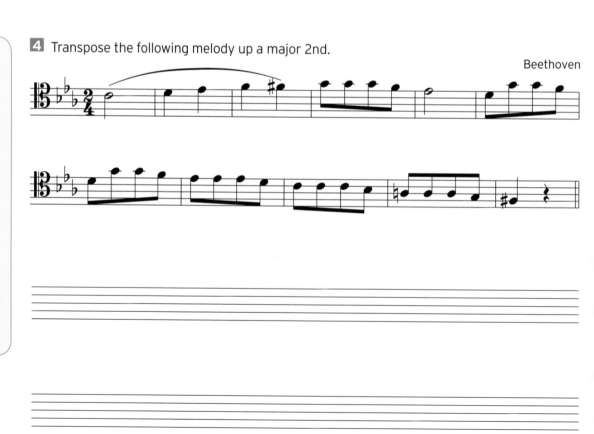

5 Transpose the following melody down a minor 3rd.

Kuhnau

6 Transpose the following melody up a minor 3rd.

Bruckner

7 Transpose the following melody down a major 3rd.

Brahms

8 Transpose the following melody up a major 3rd.

Vivaldi

9 Transpose the following melody down a perfect 4th.

Anon

10 Transpose the following melody up a perfect 4th.

Beethoven

11 Transpose the following melody down a perfect 5th.

Purcell

Remember

Music for French horn in F is written a perfect 5th higher than it sounds.

12 Transpose the following melody up a perfect 5th.

Sibelius

13 Transpose the following melody down a minor 6th.

Haydn

14 Transpose the following melody up a minor 6th.

J S Bach

etc.

Did you know?

Bracketed accidentals like the one in bar 2 are called **cautionary accidentals**. They are sometimes used to make the music easier to read.

15 Transpose the following melody down a major 6th.

Mendelssohn

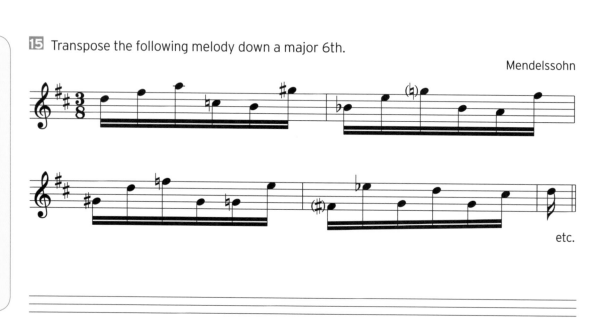

etc.

Did you know?

Music for alto saxophone in E flat is written a major 6th higher than it sounds. See page 70 for the range of this instrument.

16 Transpose the following melody up a major 6th.

Hook

17 Transpose the following melody down a minor 7th.

Schubert

18 Transpose the following melody up a minor 7th.

Bartók

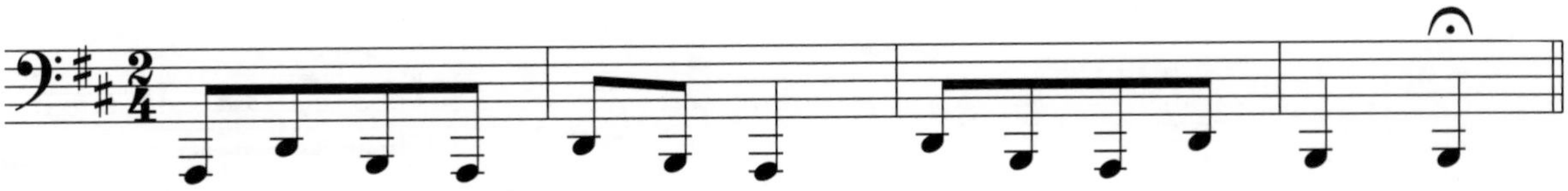

Mikrokosmos, sz 107 © Copyright 1940 by Hawkes & Son (London) Ltd. Reproduced by permission of Boosey & Hawkes Music Publishers Ltd.

19 Transpose the following melody down a major 7th.

Mozart

20 Transpose the following melody up a major 7th.

Boccherini

21 Transpose the following melody down an octave.

Mozart

22 Transpose the following melody up an octave.

Schumann

Supertonic triads

In major keys

As you know, chords I, IV and V are so important to the sound of any key that they are known as **primary chords**.

The 2nd degree (the **supertonic**) – and the triad built on it – is used less often than the primary chords but is also significant. The supertonic of the scale can also be called **re**.

Here is the scale of C major with triads built on the 1st, 2nd, 4th and 5th degrees:

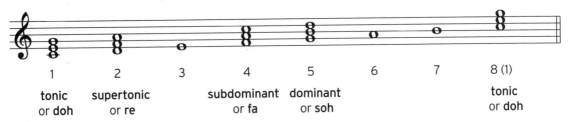

1	2	3	4	5	6	7	8 (1)
tonic or **doh**	supertonic or **re**		subdominant or **fa**	dominant or **soh**			tonic or **doh**

Here is the supertonic triad in the key of C major. Notice that it is labelled ii or Dm because the bottom interval of the triad is a minor 3rd:

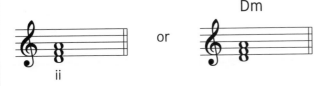

1 Here are some major scales. Write triads on the tonic, supertonic, subdominant and dominant degrees of the scale and label them with Roman numerals below the stave and chord symbols above.

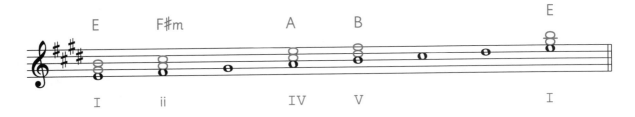

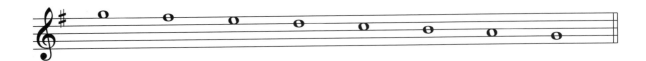

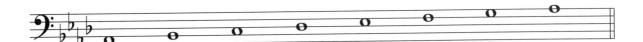

Remember

Harmony is a general word that describes the way that chord progressions work. In your exam this term could be used.

In minor keys

Supertonic triads in minor keys are built on the supertonic of the minor scale.

Here is the harmonic minor scale of A minor with triads built on the 1st, 2nd, 4th and 5th degrees:

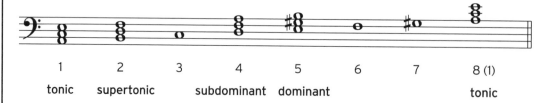

1	2	3	4	5	6	7	8 (1)
tonic	supertonic		subdominant	dominant			tonic

Here is the supertonic triad in A minor.

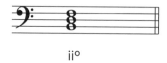

ii°

Notice that it is labelled ii because the bottom interval in the triad is a minor 3rd. However, because it also has a minor 3rd at the top (unlike chord ii in a major key), this is a **diminished triad** (shown by the circle after the Roman numeral). Play chord ii in a major and ii° in a minor key so that you can hear the difference.

Here is the way it is labelled as a chord symbol:

Bdim or B°

1 Here are some minor scales. Write triads on the tonic, supertonic, subdominant and dominant degrees of the scales and label them with Roman numerals below the stave and chord symbols above.

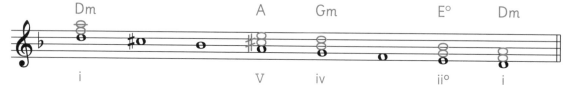

Remember

Check whether the scale is harmonic or melodic and adjust the triads as necessary. If the melodic scale is being used ii° changes back to ii because the raised 6th degree is part of the ii triad.

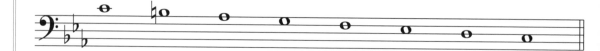

2 Circle any diminished supertonic triads.

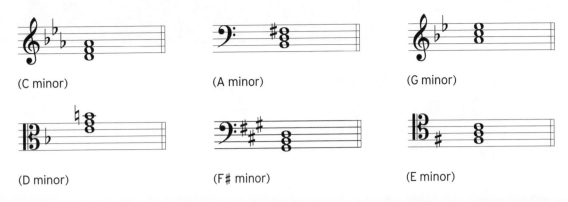

(C minor)   (A minor)   (G minor)

(D minor)   (F♯ minor)   (E minor)

Chord progression

1 Label the chords with Roman numerals below the stave and chord symbols above to show the chord progression.

Handy tip!

Notice that some of the triads are not in root position.

(C major)

(C major)

Remember

Chord progression means the order in which chords move from one to another in a piece of music.

(F major)

(E minor)

(A minor)

Writing a bass line

In major and minor keys

1 Use the root, first or second inversion bass notes of each triad shown by the Roman numerals to write a bass line. Add some repeated notes and/or octave jumps to make it interesting for the listener.

Remember

A strong bass line often moves in contrary motion to the melody. Do not let the bass line move in similar motion in perfect 5ths or octaves with the melody; this sounds weak and will lose you marks in your exam.

Traditional (English)

Traditional (Scottish)

i   V⁷   i   Vb   i   V⁷   i

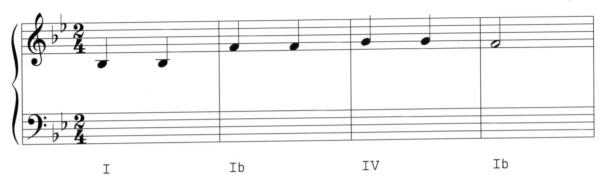

I   Ib   IV   Ib

ii   V⁷   I   Ib   iib   V⁷   I

I   Ib   IV   V   I   Ib   V

I   IV   V⁷   I

2 Use the root, first or second inversion of each triad shown by the chord symbols to write a bass line. Add some repeated notes, rests and/or octave jumps to make it interesting for the listener.

Hook

Traditional (English)

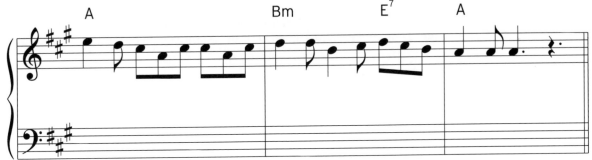

Remember

When writing passing notes in minor keys, notes from the melodic scale are often used. However, there are many cases where composers use notes from the harmonic minor scale instead; it just depends on the context and the harmony. Listen to the music you write and ask your teacher to help you decide which version is appropriate.

Accented passing notes

For Grade 4 you learned about unaccented passing notes (notes on weak beats of the bar that link harmony notes). Here is a reminder in C major:

Accented passing notes are notes that link harmony notes; but they are placed on strong beats and often clash with the harmony. Here is a reworking of the example above to show how accented passing notes are placed in the bar. This time the circled notes are accented passing notes:

Both accented and unaccented passing notes can be chromatic.

Auxiliary notes

Auxiliary notes are similar to unaccented passing notes but instead of passing from one harmony note to another, they move away from a harmony note (by a tone or semitone) and immediately return to the same one.

Here are examples of upper and lower auxiliary notes:

Upper auxiliary note

Lower auxiliary note

These can also be chromatic (upper or lower).

Here is an example of a lower chromatic auxiliary note:

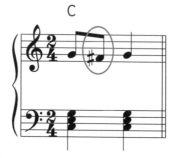

Writing a tune

1 Use notes from each chord shown by the Roman numerals to write a tune above the bass line. Decorate your tunes once you have the main harmony notes in place.

I   Ib   IV   Ib   IV   IVb   Ic   V   I

Handy tip!

For decoration you could add some passing notes, repeated notes, rests, octave jumps and/or auxiliary notes.

i   ib   iv   ii°   ib   IV   V   i

Handy tip!

Do not double the 3rd of the chord if it is already in the bass line. This sounds weak and will lose you marks in your exam.

I   IV   V   Ib   I   iib   ii   V^7 I

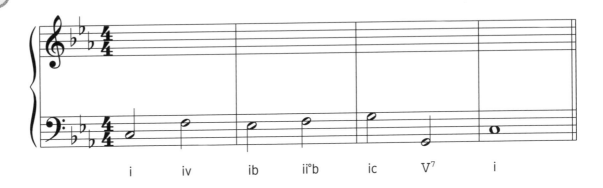

i   iv   ib   ii°b   ic   V^7 i

Remember

For decoration
you could
add some
passing notes,
repeated
notes, rests,
octave jumps
and/or
auxiliary
notes.

2 Use notes from each chord shown by the chord symbols to write a tune above the bass line. Decorate your tune once you have the main harmony notes in place.

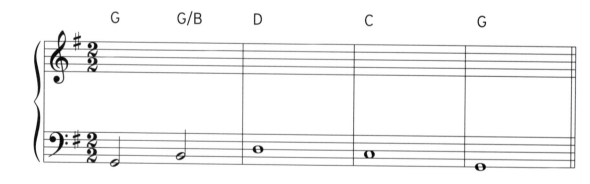

Imperfect cadences

So far you have learned to recognise perfect and plagal cadences, which composers use like punctuation in sentences. These both close on the tonic chord.

V   I

Perfect cadence

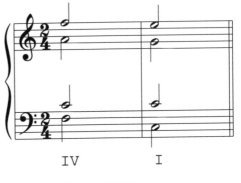

IV   I

Plagal cadence

Some cadences close on the dominant chord instead and are known as **imperfect cadences** (half-close). Here are examples of the types of imperfect cadences that you need to know for Grade 5.

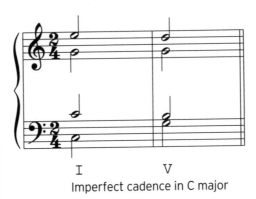

I   V

Imperfect cadence in C major

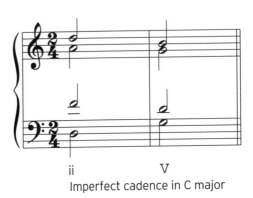

ii   V

Imperfect cadence in C major

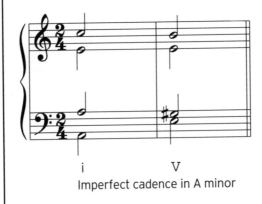

i   V

Imperfect cadence in A minor

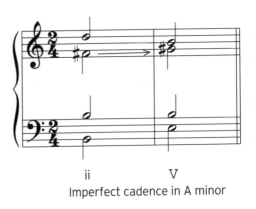

ii   V

Imperfect cadence in A minor

Remember

The 6th degree of the scale is often sharpened in minor keys where the melodic scale is used so that the contour of the voice part moves smoothly up to the leading note. If this is the case the chord is labelled ii not ii° as it would be if the harmonic minor scale were used.

1 Look at these cadences. Give the key of each cadence and say which type it is. Write in the chords in Roman numerals.

_____

_____

2 Look at these decorated cadences. Give the key of each cadence and say which type it is. Write in the chords in Roman numerals.

_____

_____

Inverting intervals

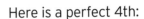

Here is a perfect 4th:

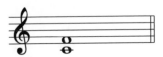

If the bottom note is put an octave higher the perfect 4th interval is **inverted** (turned upside down):

As you can see, the inversion of a perfect 4th is therefore a perfect 5th.

For Grade 5 you need to know how to invert any of the intervals covered so far and name them. The following chart shows that there is a pattern involved:

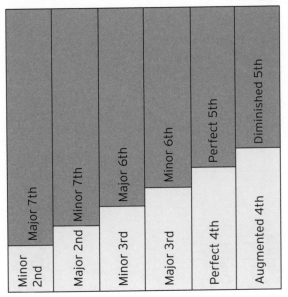

The inversion of a unison is an octave.

---

1 Name the following Grade 5 intervals. Then write their inversions and name them.

Interval: Major 7th

Inversion: Minor 2nd

Interval: _____

Inversion: _____

Interval: _____

Inversion: _____

Interval: _____   Inversion: _____

Interval: _____   Inversion: _____

Interval: _____   Inversion: _____

Interval: _____   Inversion: _____

Interval: _____   Inversion: _____

Interval: _____   Inversion: _____

Interval: _____   Inversion: _____

Interval: _____   Inversion: _____

4-part chords

Handy tip!
Play these chords on a keyboard so that you learn to imagine the sounds you write down. This will be useful when it comes to your exam.

Remember
In minor keys, check the Roman numerals to see whether the 3rd of the chord should be sharpened.

For Grade 5 you need to write tonic, supertonic, subdominant and dominant chords for SATB. You will need to know how to write them in root position, first and second inversions in the keys for the grade.

Here are some examples of the way a tonic chord in the key of A minor could be written for SATB in root position, first and second inversion:

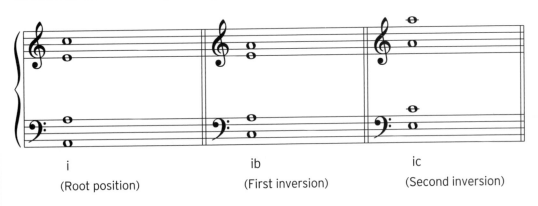

i
(Root position)

ib
(First inversion)

ic
(Second inversion)

Here are some examples of the way a dominant chord in the key of A minor might be written for SATB in root position and in first and second inversion:

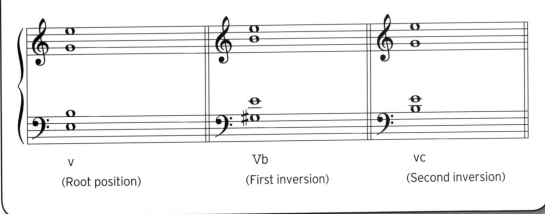

v
(Root position)

Vb
(First inversion)

Vc
(Second inversion)

1 Circle the two roots in the following chords and label each with a Roman numeral.

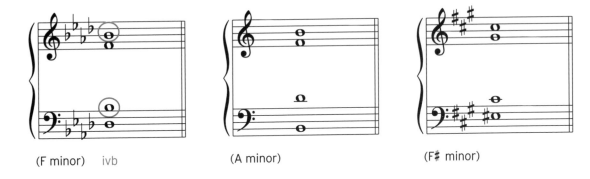

(F minor)   ivb

(A minor)

(F♯ minor)

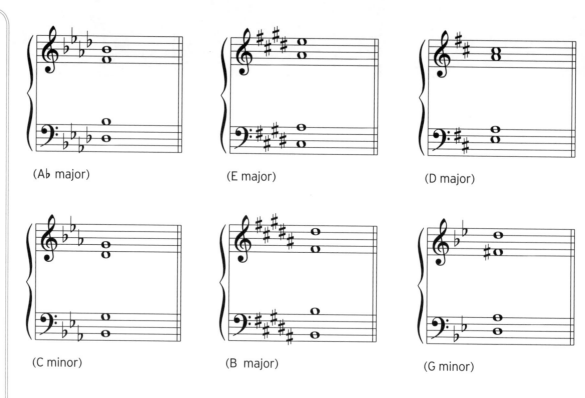

(A♭ major)   (E major)   (D major)

(C minor)   (B major)   (G minor)

2 Using crotchets, write out 4-part chords for SATB using the chords shown by the Roman numerals. Double the root in each case, even if the chord is in first or second inversion.

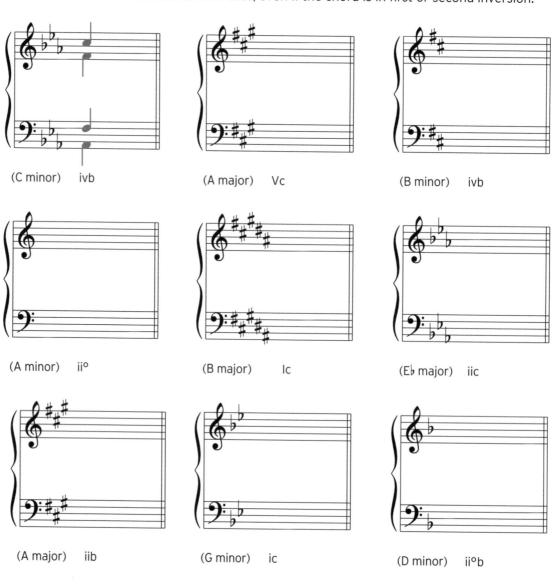

(C minor) ivb   (A major) Vc   (B minor) ivb

(A minor) ii°   (B major) Ic   (E♭ major) iic

(A major) iib   (G minor) ic   (D minor) ii°b

50

Modulation

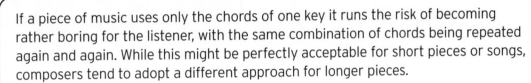

If a piece of music uses only the chords of one key it runs the risk of becoming rather boring for the listener, with the same combination of chords being repeated again and again. While this might be perfectly acceptable for short pieces or songs, composers tend to adopt a different approach for longer pieces.

Contrasting the tonic key with other keys is a good way to add interest for the listener. To do this, composers often start a piece in the tonic and then travel to related keys before returning to the tonic (also sometimes called the **home key**) Changing from one key to another is called **modulation**.

For Grade 5 you need to be able to recognise a modulation into either the relative major/minor or into the dominant major/minor key. You will be asked to find a perfect cadence in the new key and to say what relation it is to the tonic key of the piece. Look out for accidentals as clues that a modulation is about to take place.

Handy tip!
The Analysis section on page 56 will give you practice at finding where pieces modulate, but make sure that you also look for modulations in the music you play.

1 Here are some tonic chords followed by perfect cadences written in related keys. Work out what they are and the relationship between them.

Tonic chord in _C major_

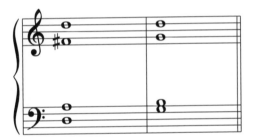

Perfect cadence in _G major_

The perfect cadence is in the _dominant major key_

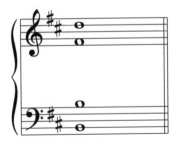

Tonic chord in _____

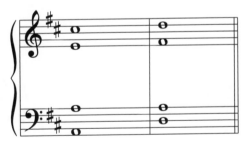

Perfect cadence in _____

The perfect cadence is in the _____

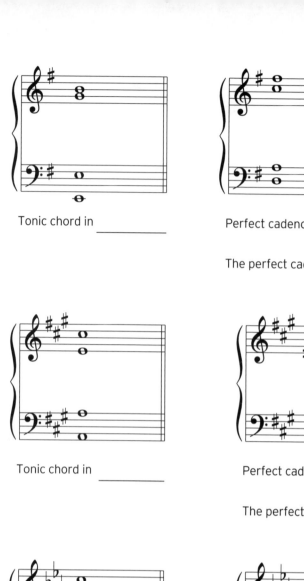

Tonic chord in _____

Perfect cadence in _____

The perfect cadence is in the _____

Tonic chord in _____

Perfect cadence in _____

The perfect cadence is in the _____

Tonic chord in _____

Perfect cadence in _____

The perfect cadence is in the _____

Tonic chord in _____

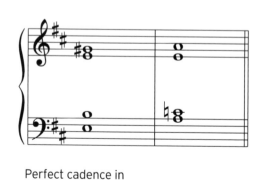

Perfect cadence in _____

The perfect cadence is in the _____

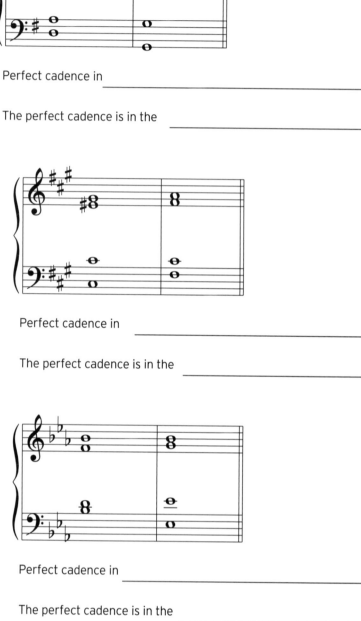

52

Musical words and symbols

Form

There are three forms that you need to be able to recognise for Grade 5: **strophic**, **verse and refrain** (or chorus and refrain) and **binary form**.

Strophic form is very commonly used in all types of songs. It is easily recognisable because the same music is used for a number of verses (with different words).

Verse and refrain form is similar to strophic form in that it uses the same music for a number of different verses, but in addition it has an unchanging refrain or chorus between each verse.

Binary form is sometimes known as AB structure because there are two sections to it (usually each A and B section is repeated so it could be written AABB).

The first section (A) usually modulates to the dominant major key (if the tonic key is major), or to the relative major (if the tonic key is minor). Its end is marked by a perfect cadence in the new key. The second section (B) is usually a bit longer than the A section. It begins in the key reached at the end of the A section and journeys through other keys back to the tonic key, generally repeating part or all of section A.

For Grade 5 you need to know the following in addition to the words and symbols for Grades 1-4.

Articulation and pedal marks (piano)

 Con pedal – the player should play with pedal (usually the right-hand one)

Senza pedal – the player should play without using the pedal

Una corda (meaning literally 'one string') – the player should play with the left pedal down (which reduces the number of strings that the hammers in the piano can strike for each note from three to one). This makes the sound much quieter than usual.

Tre corde – the player should release the left pedal (usually after an *una corda* marking) and the hammers will hit three strings again per note

 arpeggiando – quickly spread out the notes of a chord (from the bottom to the top unless marked otherwise)

Clefs

– this sign shows where music for tenor voice is written an octave higher than it sounds.

Expression marks

agitato – agitated

appassionata – with passion

con forza – with force

con fuoco – with fire

energico – with energy

morendo – dying away

risoluto – resolutely (boldly)

scherzando – playfully

sotto voce – hushed, subdued

Ornaments

(show in shorthand the way that the composer would like the tune to be further decorated)

Acciaccatura or grace note

is generally played:

Appoggiatura

This usually takes half the value of the note after it:

is generally played:

However, if it comes directly before a dotted note it can take up to two thirds of the value of the note:

is generally played:

Upper mordent

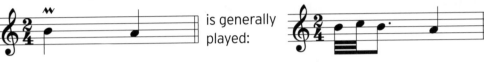

This is generally played fairly fast and is placed on the beat. If the mordent is intended to contain a sharpened or flattened note, accidentals are put above the mordent sign.

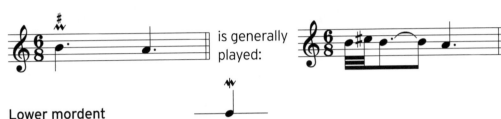

Lower mordent

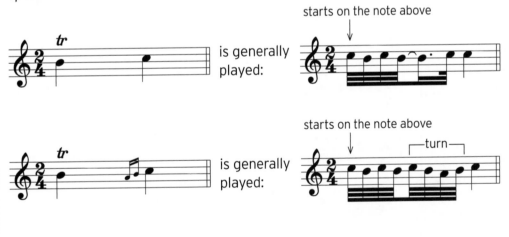

This is played as for the upper mordent but using the note below instead of the note above.

Trial or shake

tr trill

The trills that you need to know about are those used in music written before around 1800. These usually start on the note above and sometimes end with a special flourish called a 'turn'.

Tempo marks and other useful words

grave – very slow and solemn

larghetto – slowly but not as slowly as *largo*

niente – nothing

quasi – like, as if

rubato – let the tempo ebb and flow within the structure of the piece

secondo – second

stringendo – push the speed on (accelerate)

tempo giusto – in strict time

Analysis

1 Look at the following piece and answer the questions on page 58.

Did you know?

Figured bass (used in a lot of Baroque music) is based on the intervals between the bass line and the melody to be played above it.

In Baroque pieces figured bass was usually written below a melody and bass line. The keyboard player then improvised around the chord progression like a guitarist does using chord symbols. These days **realisations** of the figured bass are written in to help the player — often in small notes to show that they are just one way of interpreting the music. You are not expected to use figured bass in Grade 5.

Sinfonia

Tartini

1. In which key is this piece? _____

2. In which form is this piece composed?_____

3. To which related key has this piece modulated by bar 9?

   _____

4. Circle the first accidental that signals this modulation.

5. Rewrite the violin part in bars 23 and 24 in tenor clef.

6. Write an appropriate Roman numeral below the second crotchet beat of bar 1.

7. Write an appropriate Roman numeral below the second crotchet beat of bar 2.

8. Bracket (⌐‾‾⌐) a descending one-octave scale in the dominant key.

9. Name the interval between the two notes marked with asterisks (*) in bar 8._____

10. Comment on the pitch in bars 3 and 4 (violin part).

    _____

11. Where is bar 1 repeated a perfect 4th lower later in the piece (violin and continuo parts)?

    _____

12. Name the ornament in bar 17 (violin part).

    _____

13. On what note should the trill start in bar 24 (violin part)?_____

14. What does Largo mean?

    _____

15. Name one way the bass line is decorated.

    _____

2 Look at the following piece and answer the questions on page 61.

Lullaby

Brahms (trans. Rogers)

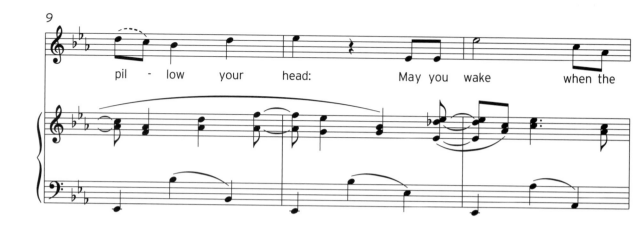

pil - low your head: May you wake when the

day Cha - ses dark - ness a - way, May you

wake when the day Cha - ses dark - ness aw - ay.

2. Lullaby and goodnight
Let angels of light
Spread wings round your bed
And guard you from dread.
Slumber gently and deep
In the dreamland of sleep,
Slumber gently and deep
In the dreamland of sleep.

1. In which key is this song?_____

2. In what form is this song composed?_____

3. Which voice (soprano, alto, tenor or bass) would be best suited to singing this song?

    _____

4. Look at the way the bass line of the piano part is written. Why do you think that it might be
    suitable to accompany this song?

    _____

    _____

5. What does *con moto, tranquillo* mean?

    _____

6. How do the dynamic markings help the mood of this song?

    _____

7. How many times is the treble part of the piano syncopated over the bar line?

    _____

8. Write an appropriate Roman numeral below the third crotchet beat of bar 17.

9. Write an appropriate Roman numeral below the first crotchet beat of bar 18.

10. Write an appropriate Roman numeral below the third crotchet beat of bar 12.

11. This song does not modulate. Name the bars where there is a hint of another key.

    _____

12. Name the interval between the two notes marked with an asterisk (*) in bar 6 (treble part).

    _____

13. Circle an interval of an augmented 4th (voice part).

14. Give two possible names for the ornament in bar 14 (voice part).

    _____

15. Why are there only 2 ½ beats in the last bar?

    _____

Sample examination paper

Section 1 (10 marks)

Put a tick (✓) in the box next to the correct answer.

Example

Name this note:

A ☐   D ☐   C ☑

This shows that you think **C** is the correct answer.

1.1   Name the circled note:

A ☐   F ☐   Eb ☐

1.2   Which is the correct grouping of main beats for this bar?

(2, 3) ☐   (3, 2) ☐   (4, 4) ☐

1.3   Which is the correct time signature?

$\frac{3}{8}$ ☐ $\frac{5}{8}$ ☐ $\frac{2}{4}$ ☐

1.4   Which note is the enharmonic equivalent of this note?

Gbb ☐   Bbb ☐   G♯ ☐

1.5   Which term does **not** refer specifically to performance by a keyboard instrument?

una corda ☐   tre corda ☐   morendo ☐

Put a tick (✓) in the box next to the correct answer.

1.6 Which note is the subdominant of the minor key shown by this key signature?

C# ☐   D ☐   B ☐

☐

1.7 The correct label for the following scale is:

F melodic minor scale ascending ☐
F natural minor scale ascending ☐
F harmonic minor scale ascending ☐

☐

1.8 Which symbol does **not** fit with this chord?

A⁷ ☐   V⁷ ☐   Am ☐

☐

1.9 Which instrument often uses this clef?

bassoon ☐   trumpet ☐   clarinet ☐

☐

1.10 Name the following:

Perfect cadence in A major ☐
Plagal cadence in A major ☐
Full close in A major ☐

☐

Section 2 (15 marks)

2.1 Write a one-octave B flat harmonic minor scale in crotchets ascending then descending. Use a key signature.

☐

63

2.2 Write the key signature of the key shown. Then write its one octave arpeggio in the rhythm
     given below.

D major going up then down

Section 3 (10 marks)

In the examination, this section may be *either* correcting mistakes *or* setting words to a rhythm.

3.1 Continue the rhythm to fit the following phrase.

In Oxford City lived a lady,
She was beautiful and fair.
She was courted by a sailor
And he did love her as his dear.

                                    - Anon.

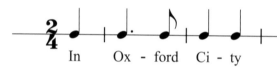

Section 4 (15 marks)

4.1 Transpose this melody up a tone so that a trumpet in B♭ will be able to play it at the same pitch as the following notes. Use a key signature.

Traditional

Section 5 (15 marks)

5.1 Using minims, write out 4-part chords for SATB using the chords shown by the Roman numerals. Double the root in each case, even if the chord is in first or second inversion.

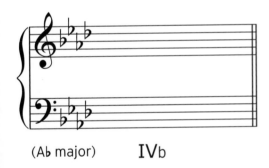

(A♭ major)   IVb

(B minor)   i

Section 6 (15 marks)

6.1 Use notes from the chords shown by the chord symbols to write a tune above the bass line. Decorate your tune once you have the main harmony notes in place.

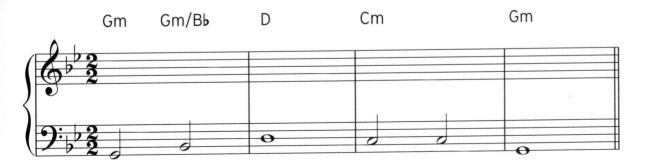

Please turn over for Section 7

Section 7 (20 marks)

Look at the following song and answer the questions on page 68.

Translation: Peter Pears

Franz Schubert

2.
Neighbours watch and neighbours listen,
Wond'ring why her windows glisten
Still among the midnight airs.
Then, O softly, softly bear it,
So that none but she may hear it;
Cheat the neighbours' greedy ears,
Cheat the neighbours' greedy ears.

7.1   In which key is this song?_____

_____

7.2   In what form is this song composed? _____

_____

7.3   What does ⅔ mean? _____

_____

7.4   Why is the composer's use of ⅔ appropriate to the words of the song (first phrase, voice part)?

_____

7.5   To which related key has the song modulated by bar 11? _____

_____

7.6   Circle the first accidental that signals this modulation (voice part).

7.7   Comment on the pitch in bars 5-8 (violin part)._____

_____

7.8   Circle the lower auxiliary note in bar 18 (voice part).

7.9   Describe the harmonic rhythm in bars 1-2. _____

_____

7.10   What kind of cadence does the composer use to finish the song?_____

_____

This page is intentionally blank, please turn over.

Instrument ranges

The ranges given here are the written ranges for players of approximately Grade 5 standard. The complete ranges (especially for string instruments) go much higher.

String instruments

 Violin

 Viola

 Cello

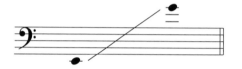 Double bass

 Classical guitar

Woodwind instruments

 Flute

 Descant recorder

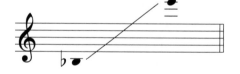 Oboe

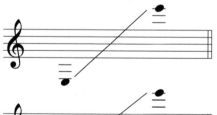 Clarinet in B flat

 Alto saxophone in E flat

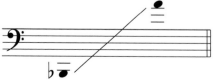 Bassoon